INTRODUCTION

A WISE MAN once shared with me the secret of creating a successful life. "It's simple," he said. "It's all in knowing what to hold close and what to flee from." I think he's right, and it's what I've learned about the values to embrace and the temptations to avoid that make up this collection and the two previous volumes of *Life's Little Instruction Book*.

Volume I began as thirty handwritten pages of fatherly advice I typed up and gave to my son, Adam, as he was beginning his freshman year at college. Two years later, I sent him another five hundred or so entries that became *Life's Little Instruction Book, Volume II*. He called me a couple of days after receiving it and indicated that he would welcome another list every two years or so. I'm right on schedule.

Adam recently graduated from college and is living in Atlanta. His mother and I visit him several times a year, and we talk regularly on the phone. More than once he's asked when *Volume III* would be ready. "Soon," I would reply, "very soon." I explained that the new collection would be different from the first two, for it would consist of observations not only from my own experiences, but also enlightening insights from other parents and grandparents as well. He then reminded me of the old proverb:

> *Good advice from one man, silver.*
> *Good advice from many men, gold.*

Adam is well on his way. He has an exciting and challenging job and in a few years will probably marry and start a family. The whole world lies before him. He's not looking for me or anyone else to pave the way, but like any wise young adventurer he welcomes advice from more experienced travelers. As his father and someone whose life's odometer is about to turn over for the second time, I

LIFE'S LITTLE INSTRUCTION BOOK™
Volume III

H. Jackson Brown, Jr.

Rutledge Hill Press®
Nashville, Tennessee
A Thomas Nelson Company

Copyright © 1995 by H. Jackson Brown, Jr.

Published by Rutledge Hill Press, a Thomas Nelson Company,
P. O. Box 141000, Nashville, Tennessee 37214.

Typography by D&T/Bailey Typesetting, Inc., Nashville, Tennessee.

Library of Congress Cataloging-in-Publication Data

Brown, H. Jackson, 1940–
    Life's little instruction book.
    1. Happiness—Quotations, maxims, etc.   2. Conduct of life—
Quotations, maxims, etc.   I. Title.
BJ1481.B87   1991   170'.44   91–9800
ISBN 1-55853-835-6 (v. 1, paperback)   ISBN 1-55853-121-1 (v. 1, hardcover)
ISBN 1-55853-836-4 (v. 2, paperback)   ISBN 1-55853-275-7 (v. 2, hardcover)
ISBN 1-55853-837-2 (v. 3, paperback)

Printed in the United States of America
1 2 3 4 5 6 7 8 9 — 05 04 03 02 01 00

delight in pointing out to him where the potholes are as well as the scenic overlooks.

My prayers go with him and all the other noble pilgrims who meet the future with bold steps and courageous hearts.

Acknowledgments

I WOULD LIKE TO THANK the following contributors for sharing their advice and insights: Christine Aitken, Lu Astrene, Donald Blackerby, Bernice Blake, Joseph J. Blank Jr., Heather Bledsoe, Brandy Blunden, Brad Brady, Jessica May Bridges, Blanche Broadbent, John R. Brubaker, Chris Burdette, Yvonne M. Burgess, Robert E. Burr, Nicole Burton, J. Bruce Camealy, H. Paul Canady III, Amanda B. Chambless, Sabrina Charles, Esther C. Chi, Timothy Cleavenger, Gary Cohen, Brenda Collins, Susan M. Condron, Lindsay Cook, LaShaunda Cox, Diane Crafts, Ovidin Cristea, Timothy Cundy, Jon Daniels, Megan E. Davis, Paul Davis, Mariken Hasert Deist, Tommy Doss, Julie Ann Dunaway, Pat Dygert, Kendall Eagan, Diane S. Emser, Joyce Evans, Maryhelen E. Evans, Carol Feneis, Charlene Fertig, Kari Lee Forde, Bonny L. Foster, Valerie Garfield, Marilyn Goodrich, Beth Grant, Josh Gray, Tobi Greer, Brandy Gregory, Kyra Harris, Matthew Hayhurst, Matthew J. Hire, Peggy Hope, Carole L. Horn, Frederick F. Hovey Jr., Chandra Howard, Amy L. Huey, Sheryl Dickson Hunnie, Emma Jane Hunt, Brandy Jackson, Wendi Jackson, Lillian Jahngen, Reid Jason, Rebecca Ellen Johnson, Cliff Jones, Susan Kaschak, Patricia A. Kebles, Katie Kerlin, Hannah Kim, Chic Klinger, Ashley C. Knowles, Grace Kolek, Nick

Books by H. Jackson Brown, Jr.

To Rosemary and Adam

1029 • Never buy a coffee table you can't put your feet on.

1030 • Say something positive as early as possible every day.

1031 • Believe in miracles but don't depend on them.

1032 • Regardless of the situation, remember that nothing is ever lost by courtesy.

1033 • Never open the refrigerator when you're bored.

1034 • Fill out expense reports the day you return from your trip.

1035 • Own at least one article of clothing with Mickey Mouse on it.

1036 • Be thankful you were born in this great country.

1037 • When staying at a hotel or motel, don't accept a room next to the ice or vending machines.

1038 • Enjoy the satisfaction that comes from doing little things well.

1039 • Never go near a kid who's holding a water hose unless you want to get wet.

1040 • Never refuse a holiday dessert.

1041 • If you are involved in an automobile accident, don't admit fault (there may be extenuating circumstances) and don't discuss the accident with anyone except the police and your insurance agent.

1042 • Encourage your children to join a choir.

1043 • Never allow anyone to intimidate you.

1044 • Watch your finances like a hawk.

1045 ◆ Don't forget that we are ultimately judged by what we give, not by what we get.

1046 ◆ Never complain about the music in someone else's car when you're a passenger.

1047 ◆ Read Tom Peter's *The Pursuit of WOW!* (Vantage, 1994).

1048 · Always compliment flower gardens and new babies.

1049 • Remember that it's better to be cheated in price than in quality.

1050 • When reading self-help books, include the Bible.

1051 • Each year, take a first-day-of-school photograph of your children.

1052 • Learn the rules of any sport your children play.

1053 ◆ When you hear a kind word spoken about a friend, tell him so.

1054 ◆ Never hesitate to do what you know is right.

1055 ◆ Pack a couple of Ziploc bags and a pad of Post-it Notes when you travel.

1056 ◆ Don't work for recognition, but do work worthy of recognition.

1057 • Share your knowledge and experiences.

1058 • Be charitable in your speech, actions, and judgment.

1059 • Work for a company where the expectations of you are high.

1060 • Don't allow your children or grandchildren to call you by your first name.

1061 • Remember that a kind word goes a long way.

1062 • Don't compare your children with their siblings or classmates.

1063 • Be enthusiastic in your expressions of gratitude and appreciation.

1064 • Ask permission before taking someone's photograph.

1065 ◆ Join the Rotary or another civic club.

1066 ◆ When no great harm will result, let your children do it their way, even if you know they are wrong. They will learn more from their mistakes than from their successes.

1067 ◆ Forgive quickly.

1068 ◆ Kiss slowly.

1069 ◆ Tell your wife often how terrific she looks.

1070 ◆ Never give an anniversary gift that has to be plugged in.

1071 ◆ Take some silly photos of yourself and a friend in an instant photo booth.

1072 ◆ Remember that regardless of where you are, not much good happens after midnight.

1073 ◆ Volunteer to be a Little League umpire.

1074 ◆ Remember that the word *discipline* means "to teach."

1075 ◆ Remember that all success comes at a price.

1076 ◆ When you give someone a camera as a gift, make sure it's loaded with film and has a battery.

1077 • Tour your state capitol building.

1078 • Own your own tuxedo.

1079 • Never say anything uncomplimentary about your wife in the presence of your children.

1080 • Remember the three universal healers: calamine lotion, warm oatmeal, and hugs.

1081 · Earn your success based
on service to others, not
at the expense of others.

1082 • Kiss your children good night, even if they are already asleep.

1083 • To fight the blues, try exercising.

1084 • Never watch a movie or video with your children that involves activities and language that you don't want them to imitate.

1085 • Learn the Heimlich maneuver.

1086 • Compliment the parent when you observe a well-behaved child.

1087 • When traveling, sleep with your wallet, car keys, room key, eyeglasses, and shoes nearby.

1088 • Spend twice as much time praising as you do criticizing.

1089 • Never pass up a chance to be in a parade.

1090 ◆ Start the standing ovation at the end of school plays.

1091 ◆ Remember the credo of Walt Disney: Think. Believe. Dream. Dare.

1092 ◆ When someone lets you down, don't give up on them.

1093 ◆ Treat your company's money as you would your own.

1094 • Remember that life's big changes rarely give advance warning.

1095 • Teach your children never to underestimate someone with a disability.

1096 • What you have to do, do wholeheartedly.

1097 • Never comment on someone's weight unless you know it's what they want to hear.

1098 • Read the *Wall Street Journal* regularly.

1099 • Find a job you love and give it everything you've got.

1100 • Keep good financial records.

1101 • Never complain about a flight delayed for mechanical repairs. Waiting on the ground is infinitely better than the alternative.

1102 ◆ Make a list of travel necessities, laminate it, and keep it in your suitcase.

1103 ◆ Set limits on the amount and content of television your children watch.

1104 ◆ Seek respect rather than popularity.

1105 ◆ Seek quality rather than luxury.

1106 ◆ Seek refinement rather than fashion.

1107 • Never forget that it takes only one person or one idea to change your life forever.

1108 • Don't hand out your troubles to your friends and co-workers.

1109 • Occasionally let your children help you, even if it slows you down.

1110 • Throw a surprise birthday party for a friend.

1111 • Always take your vacation time.

1112 • Call (800) 525-9000 for a catalog of Nightingale Conant tapes on personal development and achievement.

1113 • Start a "smile file" of jokes, articles, and cartoons that make you laugh.

1114 • Start a "read again file" for articles you might want to enjoy a second time.

1115 • When you need a little advice, call your grandparents.

1116 • Teach your sons as well as your daughters to cook.

1117 • Report unethical business practices to your city's Better Business Bureau.

1118 • Look for the opportunity that's hidden in every adversity.

1119 · Remember that when your mom says, "You'll regret it," you probably will.

1120 • Don't be critical of your wife's friends.

1121 • Be prompt when picking up or dropping off your children for school or other activities.

1122 • Don't sit while ladies are standing.

1123 • Take your teenagers with you when you buy a car or expensive household item and let them learn from the experience.

1124 ◆ Become a serious student of American history.

1125 ◆ Make a big batch of Rice Krispies squares. Take them to the office.

1126 ◆ Play catch with a kid.

1127 ◆ Write some poetry.

1128 ◆ Shoot a few hoops.

1129 • Once a month invite someone to lunch who knows more about your business than you.

1130 • Never ignore an old barking dog.

1131 • To open a bottle of champagne, twist the neck, not the cork.

1132 • To put someone in your debt, do something nice for their child.

1133 ◆ Improve even the best sausage biscuit by spreading on a little grape jelly.

1134 ◆ Try to add a new name to your Rolodex every week.

1135 ◆ If you are not going to use a discount coupon, leave it on the shelf with the product for someone else to use.

1136 ◆ Respect your elders.

1137 ◆ Never criticize your country when traveling abroad.

1138 ◆ When loved ones drive away, watch and wave until you can no longer see the car.

1139 ◆ On your birthday, send your mom a thank-you card.

1140 ◆ Never tell an off-color joke in the presence of women or children.

1141 • Keep a pad and pencil by every phone.

1142 • If you dial a wrong number, don't just hang up; offer an apology.

1143 • Spend a couple of hours each week reading magazines that have nothing to do with your job or lifestyle.

1144 • Hold yourself to the same high standards that you require of others.

1145 · Never let the odds keep
you from pursuing what
you know in your heart
you were meant to do.

1146 • Wage war against procrastination.

1147 • Don't open anyone else's mail.

1148 • If you are a guest at a wedding, take lots of snapshots and send them along with the negatives to the bride and groom as quickly as you can. They have a long time to wait for the formal pictures and will be thrilled to receive the ones you took.

1149 • Never loan your chain saw, your ball glove, or your favorite book.

1150 • Type out your favorite quotation and place it where you can see it every day.

1151 • When playing a sport with a partner, never criticize his or her performance.

1152 • Until your children move out of your house, don't buy anything suede.

1153 ◆ When the best in the world visits your town for a concert, exhibition, or speech, get tickets to attend.

1154 ◆ Learn the techniques of being a good interviewer.

1155 ◆ Listen to rumors, but don't contribute any of your own.

1156 ◆ Enter something in the state fair.

1157 ◆ Offer hope.

1158 ◆ Let your word be your bond.

1159 ◆ Count your change.

1160 ◆ Remember that a lasting marriage is built on commitment, not convenience.

1161 ◆ When you need to apologize to someone, do it in person.

1162 ◆ Try to find a copy of the book *Under My Elm* by David Grayson (Doubleday, 1942). You may have to order it.

1163 ◆ Take your child on a tour of a local university.

1164 ◆ Finish projects before they are due.

1165 ◆ Never ask a childless couple when they are going to have children.

1166 · Be happy with what you
have while working for
what you want.

1167 • Let your children observe your being generous to those in need.

1168 • Celebrate even small victories.

1169 • Never answer a reporter's questions with, "No comment." Say instead, "I don't have enough information to comment on that right now."

1170 • Cut your toenails in private.

1171 • After going to bed, refuse to worry about problems until the morning.

1172 • Return shopping carts to the designated areas.

1173 • Attend an Eagle Scout's or a Girl Scout's Golden Award induction ceremony.

1174 • Never tell a car salesman how much you want to spend.

1175 • Redeem gift certificates promptly.

1176 • Remember that a grateful heart is almost always a happy one.

1177 • Make an effort to attend weddings and funerals.

1178 • Don't forget that a couple of words of praise or encouragement can make someone's day.

1179 • Every year, send your old alma mater a few bucks.

1180 • Be especially courteous to receptionists and secretaries; they are the gate-keepers.

1181 • Make your money before spending it.

1182 • Don't overschedule your children's extracurricular activities.

1183 • Whenever you hear an ambulance siren, say a prayer for the person inside.

1184 • Worry about the consequences of the choices you make before you make them—not afterward.

1185 • Attend parent-teacher conferences and PTA meetings.

1186 • Don't take medicine in the dark.

1187 · Spoil your wife,
not your children.

1188 • Stop and look up when anyone approaches your desk.

1189 • Search out good values, but let the other guy make a fair profit on what you purchase.

1190 • Get a passport and keep it current.

1191 • Never pass up a chance to jump on a trampoline.

1192 • Be cautious of renting lodging accommodations described in the ad or brochure as "rustic."

1193 • Insist that your children complete a driver's education course at their school.

1194 • Locate the emergency exits as soon as you check into your hotel room.

1195 • Get to know your children's teachers.

1196 • Stay humble.

1197 • Stay on your toes.

1198 • Know where to find a gas station that's open twenty-four hours with a working bathroom.

1199 • Hang up on anyone you don't know who's trying to sell you a financial product over the telephone.

1200 ◆ Buy each of your children a special Christmas ornament every year. When they move into their own homes, box up the ornaments and give them as housewarming gifts.

1201 ◆ Support your local museums.

1202 ◆ Support your local symphony.

1203 ◆ Support your community college.

1204 ◆ Remember that you can miss a lot of good things in life by having the wrong attitude.

1205 • When a guest, never complain about the food, drink, or accommodations.

1206 • Take a course in public speaking.

1207 • Write a letter to the editor at least once a year.

1208 • For better security when traveling, take along a small wedge of wood and jam it under your hotel room door.

1209 • Never criticize a gift.

1210 • Never leave a loved one in anger.

1211 • Keep a roll of duct tape at home, at the office, and in your car.

1212 • Require your children to do their share of household chores.

1213 • When in doubt, smile.

1214 • Underestimate when guessing an adult's age or weight.

1215 • Overestimate when guessing someone's salary.

1216 • Choose a clothing salesperson who dresses as you wish you did.

1217 • Send notes of encouragement to military personnel and college students.

1218 • Occasionally leave a quarter in the change return slot of a pay phone. Somebody always checks.

1219 • Overpay the neighborhood kid who does yard work for you.

1220 • When a friend is in need, help him without his having to ask.

1221 • Keep an empty gas can in your trunk.

1222 • Own a salad spinner.

1223 • Own two crystal champagne glasses.

1224 • Allow drivers from out of state a little extra room on the road.

1225 • When serving hamburgers, always toast the buns.

1226 • Never whittle toward yourself.

1227 • Make a generous contribution to diabetes research.

1228 • Teach your children the pride, satisfaction, and dignity of doing any job well.

1229 • Never ask a woman when the baby is due unless you know for sure that she's pregnant.

1230 • Frame anything your child brings home on his first day of school.

1231 • Host a backyard get-together for friends and neighbors every Labor Day.

1232 • Keep $10 in your glove box for emergencies.

1233 • Volunteer to help at your city's Special Olympics.

1234 · Never be too busy to meet someone new.

1235 ◆ Remember that cruel words deeply hurt.

1236 ◆ Remember that loving words quickly heal.

1237 ◆ Surprise someone who's more than eighty years old or a couple celebrating fifty years or more of marriage with a personal greeting from the President. Mail details to The White House, Greetings Office, Room 39, Washington, DC 20500, four to six weeks in advance.

1238 ◆ If it's not a beautiful morning, let your cheerfulness make it one.

1239 ◆ Plant a tree the day your child is born.

1240 ◆ Toss in a coin when passing a wishing well.

1241 ◆ Don't say anything on a cordless or cellular telephone that you don't want the world to hear.

1242 ◆ Never get yourself into a position where you have to back up a trailer.

1243 ◆ Marry someone your equal or a little bit better.

1244 ◆ Keep a special notebook. Every night before going to bed, write down something beautiful that you saw during the day.

1245 ◆ When you're the first one up, be quiet about it.

1246 ◆ This year, visit two or three of your state parks.

1247 ◆ Remember that a minute of anger denies you sixty seconds of happiness.

1248 ◆ Include a recent family photo when writing to a loved one.

1249 • Ask your grandparents to tell you stories about your parents while they were growing up.

1250 • Become a Big Brother or Big Sister.

1251 • Welcome the unexpected! Opportunities rarely come in neat, predictable packages.

1252 • Before criticizing a new employee, remember your first days at work.

1253 · To help your children turn out well, spend twice as much time with them and half as much money.

1254 • Give young children the opportunity to participate in family decision-making; their insight will surprise you.

1255 • Tell family members you love them before they go away for a few days.

1256 • Keep a backup copy of your personal address and telephone book.

1257 • Fill out customer comment cards.

1258 ◆ Mail in your Publishers Clearing House sweepstakes notice. Who knows?

1259 ◆ Don't make eating everything on their plate an issue with children.

1260 ◆ Never miss an opportunity to go fishing with your father.

1261 ◆ Never miss an opportunity to go traveling with your mother.

1262 ◆ Hold a child's hand when crossing the street.

1263 ◆ Do something every day that maintains your good health.

1264 ◆ Every spring set out a couple of tomato plants.

1265 ◆ When traveling, stop occasionally at local cafés and diners.

1266 • Never deny anyone the opportunity to do something nice for you.

1267 • Never tell a woman you liked her hair better before she had it cut.

1268 • When playing golf and tennis, occasionally play with someone better than you are.

1269 • Dust, then vacuum.

1270 • Offer to pay for parking and tolls when you ride with someone.

1271 • Offer to leave the tip when someone invites you out to eat.

1272 • Visit a pet store every once in a while and watch the children watch the animals.

1273 • Remember that a successful future begins right now.

1274 • Don't minimize your child's worries and fears.

1275 • Take advantage of free lectures on any subject in which you are remotely interested.

1276 • Never give up on a dream just because of the length of time it will take to accomplish it. The time will pass anyway.

1277 • Use good stationery when you want your written comments to be taken seriously.

1278 • Unless it creates a safety problem, pull your car over and stop when a funeral procession is passing.

1279 • Be the first adult to jump into the pool or run into the ocean with the kids. They will love you for it.

1280 · Hold puppies, kittens, and babies any time you get the chance.

1281 • Ask your boss what he expects of you.

1282 • Don't play your car stereo so loud that you can't hear approaching emergency vehicles.

1283 • Memorize the names of the books of the Bible.

1284 • Memorize the names and order of the Presidents.

1285 • Take Trivial Pursuit cards to read to the driver on a long road trip. It makes the time fly.

1286 • After children argue and have said their "I'm sorrys," ask each one to say something nice about the other.

1287 • Never forget the debt you owe to all those who have come before you.

1288 ◆ Watch your back.

1289 ◆ Watch your weight.

1290 ◆ Watch your language.

1291 ◆ Remember that anything creative and innovative will be copied.

1292 ◆ When traveling, pack more underwear and socks than you think you will need.

1293 • Dress for the position you want, not the one you have.

1294 • Keep a couple of your favorite inspirational books by your bedside.

1295 • Don't write down anything you don't want someone else to read.

1296 • Whisper in your sleeping child's ear, "I love you."

1297 • At least once in your life, see the Grand Teton Mountains from the back of a horse.

1298 • Never ignore a ringing fire alarm.

1299 • When taking a true-false test, remember that any statement that includes the word *any, all, always, never,* or *ever* is usually false.

1300 • Let your children know that regardless of what happens, you'll always be there for them.

1301 • Keep a blanket in the trunk of your car for emergencies during the winter months.

1302 • Take a ride in a glider.

1303 • Take a ride in a hot-air balloon.

1304 • Be the first to apologize to a family member after a disagreement.

1305 • To find out who is behind an idea or activity, follow the money.

1306 • If you borrow something more than twice, buy one for yourself.

1307 • When you build a home, make sure it has a screened-in porch.

1308 • Be innovative.

1309 • Be passionate.

1310 • Be committed.

1311 • Become knowledgeable about antiques, oriental rugs, and contemporary art.

1312 • Don't get caught glancing at your watch when you're talking to someone.

1313 · Remember that life's most treasured moments often come unannounced.

1314 • Never tell anybody they can't sing.

1315 • Never tell anybody they don't have a sense of humor.

1316 • Call a radio talk show with an opinion.

1317 • When parents introduce you to their children, say, "I have looked forward to meeting you, because your parents are always bragging about you."

1318 • Don't argue with your mother.

1319 • Clear the adding machine after using it.

1320 • Before buying that all-important engagement ring, find out all you can about diamonds by calling (800) 340-3028. The American Gem Society will send you a booklet that will answer some of your questions.

1321 • Every December, give the world a precious gift. Give a pint of blood.

1322 • Plant a couple of fruit trees in your back yard.

1323 • Wear a tie with cartoon characters on it if you work with kids.

1324 • Remember that every age brings new opportunities.

1325 ◆ Know your children's friends.

1326 ◆ Eat lightly or not at all before giving a speech or making a presentation.

1327 ◆ Attend family reunions and be patient when aunts and uncles want to take your picture.

1328 ◆ Go for long, hand-holding walks with your wife.

1329 ◆ Visit the Biltmore estate in Asheville, North Carolina, during the spring tulip festival.

1330 ◆ Ask an older person you respect to tell you his or her proudest moment and greatest regret.

1331 ◆ Record the birthday heights of your children on the kitchen doorjamb. Never paint it.

1332 • Every once in a while, let your kids play in the rain.

1333 • When a woman is in the hospital, give her a soft, stuffed animal instead of flowers.

1334 • Always order bread pudding when it's on the menu.

1335 • Create and maintain a peaceful home.

1336 · Become the world's most thoughtful friend.

1337 • Never ask anyone why they wear a Medic Alert bracelet. That's his or her business.

1338 • Tell gardeners of public areas how much you appreciate the beauty they bring to your city.

1339 • When taking family photos, include a few routine, everyday shots.

1340 ◆ Remember that anything worth doing is going to take longer than you think.

1341 ◆ No matter how angry you get with your wife, never sleep apart.

1342 ◆ Carry a kite in the trunk for windy spring days.

1343 ◆ Buy a flashlight for each person in your family to keep in their bedroom.

1344 ◆ Never marry someone in hopes that they'll change later.

1345 ◆ Own a world globe.

1346 ◆ Own a good set of encyclopedia.

1347 ◆ Teach a Sunday school class.

1348 ◆ Never call anybody stupid, even if you're kidding.

1349 • Find something that's important to your company and learn to do it better than anyone else.

1350 • Don't eat anything covered with chocolate unless you know what's inside.

1351 • Don't eat anything covered with gravy unless you know what's under it.

1352 • Don't drink anything blue.

1353 • Even when traveling on vacation, always pack a white dress shirt and a tie.

1354 • Keep a photograph of each person you have dated.

1355 • Keep a current city and state highway map in your car's glove box.

1356 • Buy your mom flowers and your dad a new tie with your first paycheck.

1357 • Be prudent.

1358 • Be positive.

1359 • Be polite.

1360 • Ever wonder what it takes to become an astronaut? Receive the application package by writing to NASA, Johnson Space Center, Attn: AHX Astronaut Selection Office, Houston, TX 77059.

1361 ◆ If you live in the same city as your mother-in-law, occasionally trim her hedges and wash her car.

1362 ◆ Don't buy cheap picture frames.

1363 ◆ Don't buy a cheap tennis racket.

1364 ◆ Don't buy a cheap motorcycle helmet.

1365 ◆ Criticize the behavior, not the person.

1366 ✦ Never leave fun to find fun.

1367 ✦ When traveling, carry the phone
number and address of your
destination in your wallet.

1368 ✦ Collect seashells from your favorite
beach.

1369 ✦ Collect menus from your favorite
restaurants.

1370 · Rebuild a broken relationship.

1371 ◆ Notify the manager when a restaurant's restroom isn't clean.

1372 ◆ On long-distance road trips, make sure that someone besides the driver stays awake.

1373 ◆ Treat yourself to a professional shoeshine the next time you're at the airport.

1374 • At least once a month, get real dirty and sweaty.

1375 • Ask your child to read a bedtime story to you for a change.

1376 • Play Monopoly with your in-laws. It will reveal a lot about them.

1377 • Give a trusted auto technician all your repairs, not just the tough ones.

1378 ◆ Write a letter of encouragement to the President—even if he didn't get your vote.

1379 ◆ Find a creative florist and give them all your business.

1380 ◆ Buy an inexpensive Polaroid camera. Sometimes you don't want to wait an hour to see the pictures.

1381 ✦ Send Valentines to your children as well as to your wife.

1382 ✦ When eating either cinnamon rolls or prime rib, eat the center first.

1383 ✦ Add postscripts to your letters. Make them sweet and kind.

1384 ✦ Remember that bad luck as well as good luck seldom lasts long.

1385 • Never let anyone challenge you to drive faster than you think is safe.

1386 • Stop at the visitor's information center when entering a state for the first time.

1387 • When you see someone sitting alone on a bench, make it a point to speak to them.

1388 • Keep receipts.

1389 ◆ Wet your hands before lifting a trout from the river.

1390 ◆ Don't force machinery.

1391 ◆ When walking a dog, let the dog pick the direction.

1392 ◆ Teach your children that when they divide anything, the other kid gets first pick.

1393 • Offer your place in line at the grocery checkout if the person behind you has only two or three items.

1394 • Never give a friend's or relative's name or phone number to a telephone solicitor.

1395 • When going to buy a car, leave your good watch at home.

1396 ◆ Don't be so open-minded that your brains fall out.

1397 ◆ Learn to make corn bread in a cast-iron skillet.

1398 ◆ Stand up when an elderly person enters the room.

1399 ◆ Put a love note in your wife's luggage before she leaves on a trip.

1400 · Exercise caution the first day you buy a chain saw. You'll be tempted to cut down everything in the neighborhood.

1401 ✦ Never buy an article of clothing thinking it will fit if you lose a couple of pounds.

1402 ✦ Root for your team to win, not for the other team to lose.

1403 ✦ Buy an extra box of Girl Scout cookies.

1404 ✦ Be grateful that God doesn't answer all your prayers.

1405 • Accept triumph and defeat with equal grace.

1406 • Always watch the high school bands' halftime performances. They practiced just as hard as the football teams.

1407 • Never set a drink down on a book.

1408 • Eat at a truck stop.

1409 • Listen to your favorite music while working on your tax return.

1410 • Sniff an open bottle of suntan lotion and a fresh lime to temporarily curb the winter blues.

1411 • Never give a pet as a surprise gift.

1412 • When a child is selling something for a dime, give a quarter.

1413 • Never ignore an oil warning light.

1414 • After someone apologizes to you, don't lecture them.

1415 • When you move into a new house, plant a rosebush and put out a new welcome mat to make it seem like home.

1416 • Make your wedding anniversary an all-day celebration.

1417 • Blow a kiss when driving away from loved ones.

1418 • Carry a couple of inexpensive umbrellas in your car that you can give to people caught in the rain.

1419 • Be willing to accept a temporary inconvenience for a permanent improvement.

1420 • When you complete a course, shake the instructor's hand and thank him or her.

1421 • Contribute something to each Salvation Army kettle you pass during the holidays.

1422 • If you ever own rental property, remember that an unrented house is better than a bad tenant.

1423 · Never order barbecue in a restaurant where all the chairs match.

1424 ◆ Carry a small Swiss Army knife on your key chain.

1425 ◆ When you really like someone, tell them. Sometimes you only get one chance.

1426 ◆ Never make fun of people who speak broken English. It means they know another language.

1427 • When going through the checkout line, always ask the cashier how she's doing.

1428 • Take more pictures of people than of places.

1429 • Learn and use the four-digit extension to your ZIP code.

1430 • When you need something done, ask a busy person.

1431 • Call three friends on Thanksgiving and tell them how thankful you are for their friendship.

1432 • Read acknowledgments, introductions, and prefaces to books.

1433 • Never underestimate the influence of the people you have allowed into your life.

1434 • Send a "thinking of you" card to a friend who's experiencing the anniversary of the loss of a loved one.

1435 • Learn your great-grandparents' names and what they did.

1436 • Enter a room or meeting like you own the place.

1437 • Refinish a piece of furniture. Just once.

1438 • Don't use your teeth to open things.

1439 • When you are angry with someone who means a lot to you, write a letter telling him or her why you feel that way—but don't mail it.

1440 • Occasionally walk through old cemeteries and read the gravestones.

1441 • Never keep a free ride waiting.

1442 • Savor every day.

1443 • If you ask someone to do something for you, let them do it their way.

1444 • Once a year take your boss to lunch.

1445 • Wave to train engineers.

1446 • Be able to recommend three or four free hometown "must sees."

1447 · Protect your enthusiasm from the negativity of others.

1448 • When visiting state and national parks, take advantage of all tours and lectures given by park rangers.

1449 • Call your parents when you return from a long trip.

1450 • Catch up on the bestsellers by listening to books on tape in your car.

1451 • Learn to paddle a canoe.

1452 • When someone you know is down and out, mail them a twenty-dollar bill anonymously.

1453 • Share the remote control.

1454 • When pouring something from one container to another, do it over the sink.

1455 • Aspirin is aspirin. Buy the least expensive brand.

1456 • Never go up a ladder with just one nail.

1457 • Remember the best way to improve your kids is to improve your marriage.

1458 • When moving from a house or apartment, for nostalgia's sake, take a photo of each room while the furniture is still in place.

1459 • Stand out from the crowd.

1460 ◆ Don't spend lots of time with couples who criticize each other.

1461 ◆ Once in your life, paint a picture.

1462 ◆ Never buy a Rolex watch from someone who is out of breath.

1463 ◆ Never fry bacon while naked.

1464 ◆ Never squat with your spurs on.

1465 • Pay attention to pictures of missing children.

1466 • Read biographies of successful men and women.

1467 • Remember, it's not your job to get people to like you, it's your job to like people.

1468 • Offer to say grace at holiday meals.

1469 • Never miss a chance to shake hands with Santa.

1470 • When someone gives you something, never say, "You shouldn't have."

1471 • Remember that the only dumb question is the one you wanted to ask but didn't.

1472 • Watch a video on CPR and emergency first aid with your family.

1473 · Ask yourself if what you're doing today is getting you closer to where you want to be tomorrow.

1474 • When you find a coin on the ground, pick it up and give it to the first person you see.

1475 • Add *The Book of Virtues* by William Bennett (Simon & Schuster, 1993) to your home library.

1476 • Don't expect different results from the same behavior.

1477 ◆ Spend time with lucky people.

1478 ◆ Always offer guests something to eat or drink when they drop by.

1479 ◆ Make your bed every morning.

1480 ◆ Wash whites separately.

1481 ◆ Keep a couple of Wet-Naps in the glove box.

1482 • Never date anyone who has more than two cats.

1483 • Treat your parents to a dinner out on your birthday.

1484 • Don't look through other people's medicine cabinets, closets, or refrigerators.

1485 • Hug a cow.

1486 • When someone tells you they love you, never say, "No, you don't."

1487 • When you race your kids, let them win at the end.

1488 • Once a summer, run through a yard sprinkler.

1489 • Experience a real adventure: float the Gauley River in West Virginia.

1490 ◆ Remember that nothing important was ever achieved without someone's taking a chance.

1491 ◆ Stand up for your high principles even if you have to stand alone.

1492 ◆ Watch reruns of *The Wonder Years*.

1493 ◆ Every couple of months, spend thirty minutes or so in a big toy store.

1494 · Never resist a generous impulse.

1495 · When babies are born into your family, save the newspaper from that day. Give it to them on their eighteenth birthday.

1496 · Support family businesses.

1497 · Carefully examine your written work when you are finished.

1498 · Even on short ferry rides, always get out of your car and enjoy the crossing.

1499 ◆ Write a thank-you note to your children's teacher when you see your child learning new things.

1500 ◆ When on vacation or a family holiday, don't be too concerned about the cost. This is not a time to count pennies; it's a time to make memories.

1501 ◆ Be faithful.

1502 • Read the *Old Farmer's Almanac*.

1503 • Remember that everyone has bad days.

1504 • Learn to eat with chopsticks.

1505 • Make sure the telephone number on your letterhead and business cards is large enough to read easily.

1506 • Never sharpen a boomerang.

1507 • Never intentionally embarrass anyone.

1508 • Question your prejudices.

1509 • Eat moderately.

1510 • Exercise vigorously.

1511 • When you're angry, take a thirty-minute walk; when you're really angry, chop some firewood.

1512 • Be wary of stopping at restaurants displaying Help Wanted signs.

1513 • When returning a book or an item of clothing you have borrowed, leave a note of appreciation.

1514 • When you pass a family riding in a big U-Haul truck, give them the "thumbs-up" sign. They need all the encouragement they can get.

1515 ◆ Have your piano tuned every six months.

1516 ◆ Avoid automated teller machines at night.

1517 ◆ Add *Art of the Western World* to your videocassette collection.

1518 ◆ Remember the main thing is to keep the main thing the main thing.

1519 • Have your pastor over for dinner.

1520 • Marry someone who loves music.

1521 • Learn the history of your hometown.

1522 • Take your family to a dude ranch for a vacation.

1523 • See any detour as an opportunity to experience new things.

1524 • When adults are sick, care for them as though they were children.

1525 • Watch what you eat at cocktail parties. Each hors d'oeuvre has about one hundred calories.

1526 • Remember that wealth is not having all the money you want, but having all the money you need.

1527 • When deplaning, thank the captain for a safe and comfortable flight.

1528 • Never break off communications with your children, no matter what they do.

1529 • Have a little money in the bank to handle unforeseen problems.

1530 • Read *Growing a Business* by Paul Hawken (Simon & Schuster, 1987).

1531 ◆ Remember that much truth is spoken in jest.

1532 ◆ Don't forget that your attitude is just as important as the facts.

1533 ◆ Visit the Art Institute of Chicago.

1534 ◆ Take a course in basic car repair.

1535 ◆ Take your dad bowling.

1536 · Don't live with
the brakes on.

1537 ◆ Never complain about the food or entertainment at church suppers or charity functions.

1538 ◆ When talking to someone who's a new parent, always ask to see a picture of the baby.

1539 ◆ Remember that true happiness comes from virtuous living.

1540 • Don't obligate yourself to a home mortgage larger than three times your family's annual income.

1541 • When asked, take the time to give out-of-town visitors complete and clear directions.

1542 • Pass down family recipes.

1543 • Talk to your plants.

1544 • Ask for advice when you need it, but remember that no one is an expert on your life.

1545 • If you know you're going to lose, do it with style.

1546 • Say something every day that encourages your children.

1547 • Rescue your dreams.

1548 ◆ Remember that creating a successful marriage is like farming; you have to start over again every morning.

1549 ◆ Teach by example.

1550 ◆ Commit yourself to a mighty purpose.

1551 ◆ Live simply.

1552 ◆ Think quickly.

1553 • Work diligently.

1554 • Fight fairly.

1555 • Give generously.

1556 • Laugh loudly.

1557 • Love deeply.

1558 • Plant more flowers than you pick.

1559 • Remember that all important truths are simple.

1560 • Include your parents in your prayers.

Dear Reader,

If you received advice from your parents or grandparents that was especially meaningful and you would like me to share it with other readers, please write and tell me about it.

I look forward to hearing from you.

H. Jackson Brown, Jr.
P.O. Box 150155
Nashville TN 37215